Animal World

Butterflies

Donna Bailey and Christine Butterworth

STECK-VAUGHN
L I B R A R Y
A Division of Steck-Vaughn Company

Have you seen butterflies in your garden?
Butterflies like to come out when
it is sunny.
They visit the sweet-smelling plants
and flowers.

2

This is a Tortoiseshell butterfly.
It opens its wings to warm them
in the sun.
Look at the pretty patterns on its wings.

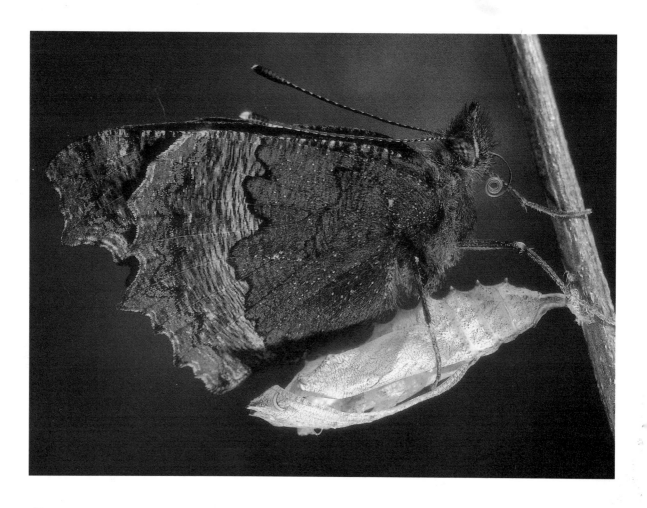

Can you see the butterfly's tongue?
It is curled up under its head.
The butterfly uncurls its tongue to drink
the sweet nectar from a flower.

The tongue is like a long tube.
The butterfly sucks the nectar up the tube.
This is just like drinking through a straw!

Butterflies have long feelers
with knobs on the ends of them.
Butterflies use their feelers
to smell and to taste things.

Male and female butterflies find
each other by their smell.
Then they mate on a leaf.

The female butterfly lands on a nettle.
She lays her eggs on a leaf.

When the eggs hatch, a tiny caterpillar
comes out of each egg.
These caterpillars like eating nettle leaves.
They have strong jaws and can eat a lot!

The caterpillar grows bigger, but
its skin does not grow. It splits.
The caterpillar sheds its old skin.
It has grown a new one underneath.

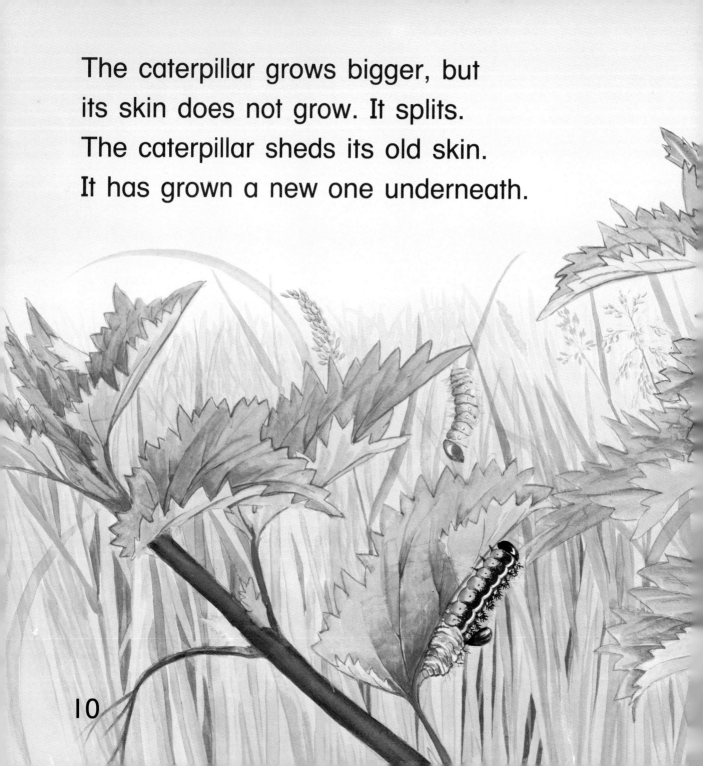

The caterpillar sheds its skin four times.
After a month, it is fully grown.
Now it finds a quiet place.
It is going to change its shape.

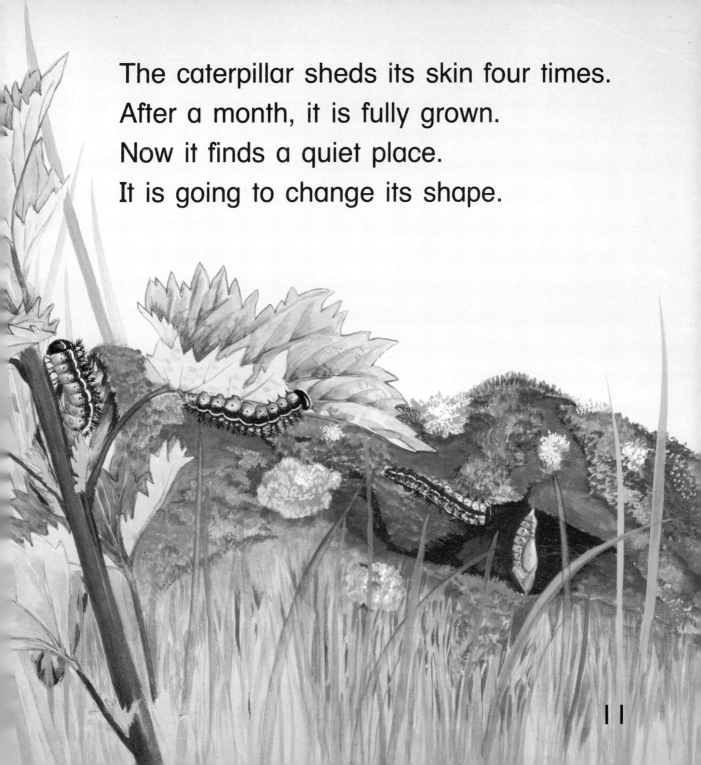

The caterpillar spins a silk thread from
its tail to tie itself to a stalk.
Then its skin turns hard.
The caterpillar turns into a pupa.

12

When the caterpillar is inside the pupa,
it changes into a butterfly.
Can you see the wings growing
inside this pupa?

One warm summer's day the new butterfly
comes out of the pupa.
Its wings are still crumpled and wet.
The butterfly rests in the sun
until its wings are dry.

Most butterflies have colors on top
of their wings.
The undersides of their wings are
plain and dull.
This helps the butterflies to hide
from their enemies when they are resting.

There are thousands of different kinds
of butterflies in the world.
They live in gardens, in forests,
and in grasslands.
They probably live near you!

There are thousands of different kinds
of butterflies and moths in the world.
They live in gardens, in forests
and in grasslands.
The butterflies in our picture
live in Africa.

These are Monarch butterflies.
In the summer they live in
North America.
When autumn comes and it gets cold,
crowds of them fly south.

The Monarch butterflies spend the winter
in Mexico where it is warm.
In the spring they fly back to the north.
They use the same route that they took
to fly south.

This Birdwing butterfly is
the largest butterfly in the world.
Its wings are 11 inches across.
It lives in forests where it is very hot.

Most butterflies have lovely colors
on their wings.
The colors on the wings of this butterfly
warn birds that it is not good to eat.

This butterfly is a Purple Emperor.
Its wings shine brightly in the sun.

A butterfly's wing is covered with
tiny scales of different colors.
These scales shine in the light.
They are very delicate.

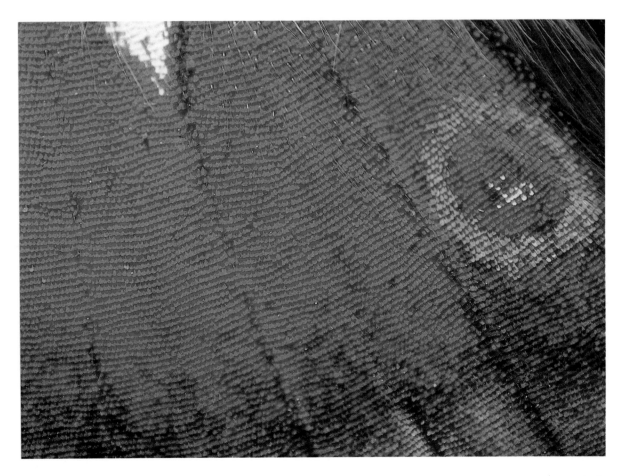

Some butterflies use the colors on
their wings to hide from their enemies.
This butterfly has pretty colors on
the top of its wings.

When its wings are folded together
it looks like a dead leaf.
It is called a Dead Leaf butterfly.
Can you see it in the picture?

Other butterflies have bold patterns
on their wings to frighten their
enemies away.
The patterns on the wings of this
Owl butterfly look like the eyes of an owl.

Moths also use patterns to frighten
their enemies.
If a bird comes too close, this Hawk moth
flashes the spots on its wings.
It frightens the bird away.

Moths are like butterflies, but
most moths have dull colors
on their wings.
Their bodies are thicker and more hairy.

Moths fold their wings flat on
their bodies when they rest.
A butterfly folds it wings together
above its body.

Moths do not have knobs on
their feelers like butterflies.
Their feelers are straight and thin.

Butterflies fly by day, but
most moths fly at night.
They use their feelers to
smell their way in the dark.

Look at this Death's Head moth.
Can you see the pattern of
a skull on its back?
It makes the moth look very fierce
and dangerous to its enemies.
But butterflies and moths are harmless.

Index

Birdwing butterfly 20

bodies 28, 29

caterpillars 9, 10, 11, 12, 13

colors 15, 21, 23, 24, 28

Dead Leaf butterfly 25

Death's Head moth 16

eggs 8, 9

feelers 6, 30, 31

flying 19, 31

Hawk moth 27

jaws 9

mating 7

Monarch butterflies 18, 19

nectar 4, 5

Owl butterfly 26

patterns 3, 26, 27, 32

pupa 12, 13, 14

Purple Emperor butterfly 22

scales 23

skin 10, 11, 12

smell 6, 7, 31

taste 6

tongue 4, 5

Tortoiseshell butterfly 3

wings 3, 13, 14, 15, 16, 20, 21, 22, 23, 24, 25, 26, 27, 28, 29

Reading Consultant: Diana Bentley
Editorial Consultant: Donna Bailey
Supervising Editor: Kathleen Fitzgibbon

Illustrated by Paula Chasty
Picture research by Suzanne Williams
Designed by Richard Garratt Design

Photographs
Cover: NHPA/Stephen Dalton
Bruce Coleman: 8 (Kim Taylor)
Frank Lane Picture Agency: 2 (M. J. Thomas), 6 (Peggy Heard), 18 (Ron
    Austing), 26 (Roger Wilmshurst), 27 (Martin Withers)
Eric and David Hosking: 15 and 32
NHPA: 3 and 7 (N. A. Callow), 4 (G. J. Cambridge), 13, 14 and 29 (Stephen
    Dalton), 19 (James Carmichael), 20 (L. H. Newman), 21 (N. J. Dennis),
    23 (G. Bernard), 28 (M. W. F. Tweedie)
OSF Picture Library: title page, 5, 9, 12 and 17 (G. I. Bernard), 16 (G. A.
    Maclean), 22 (J. S. & E. J. Wolmer), 24 and 25 (Animals Animals)

Library of Congress Cataloging-in-Publication Data: Bailey, Donna. Butterflies/Donna Bailey and Christine Butterworth;
[illustrated by Paula Chasty]. p. cm.—(Animal world) SUMMARY: Discusses the characteristics of several butterflies and th
differences between moths and butterflies. ISBN 0-8114-2635-1 1. Butterflies—Juvenile literature. [1. Butterflies. 2. Moths
I. Butterworth, Christine. II. Chasty, Paula, ill. III. Title. IV. Series: Animal world (Austin, Tex.) QL544.2.B35 1990
595.78'9—dc20 89-22016 CIP AC